A Bottle of Red

Anna Kang

Published by And Then Press, 2025.

A BOTTLE OF RED

First edition. June 26, 2025.

Copyright © 2025 Anna Kang.

ISBN: 979-8991833875

Written by Anna Kang.

Table of Contents

To Sylvia and Rosemary

A Word from the Poet

It's been over forty years since I immigrated to Sydney. I am a Korean Australian poet.

In the poem *You and I are*, I reflect on the division between South and North Korea. It's been more than seventy years since countless families were separated, and I wrote the poem to hold that long sorrow.

Letting go of war and politics, I look into the world of a father, the head of a family.
I recall my own father, sitting in a small room surrounded by four walls, staring at a hopeless *Wall*
while drawing up hopeful plans for his family's future.

One day, quite suddenly,
not even realizing spring had come,
I saw *The Cornelian Cherry* blossoms and thought,
"Ah... so it's spring,"
and in that moment, the children moved forward with their lives,
tasting *The Joy of Being One*.

Even though *Life* offers no clear answers,
I paddle my little boat in search of friendship.
That boat drifts beneath the rising sun at *Nelson Bay Beach*,
missing the mountains and streams of home,

until a wave becomes a brush
and paints a Hibiscus syriacus blossom on the rocks.

Before I know it, it's autumn.
When I long for the narrow paths of home lined with *The Cosmos* flowers,
I find myself lost in the thought:
perhaps those cosmos wear rainbow hanbok
and are counting stars on an autumn night.

That longing becomes heartache,
and heartache becomes *The Resurrection Lilies* blooming on the hillside.
Leaning there, I gaze toward the sky over my homeland,
hoping to feel the wind blowing from that direction,
but who could truly know such a feeling?

I stand in that wind and look toward mist-covered peaks.
On a day of summer rain, a woman's nobility blossoms like the *Blue Plum* flowers.
Her life, like a bush warbler
perched on a thin branch,
never ceases its quiet lament.

Then, in an instant, she scatters in the wind, becoming tears.
Meanwhile, her daughter enters college,
and sitting beside *Camellias* in the winter wind,
she begins to learn a love
as pure and deep as falling snow.

And now, as I gaze at the red twilight,

I reflect on the sorrows and joys of life.
Recalling the people who shaped our world
and the histories they forged,
the evening sky quietly stains the life of a writer lost in thought,
and the clink of red wine glasses echoes with poetic resonance.

I want to share my poetry with those who love poetry.
As you read this book, I hope you feel both joy and warmth.

And finally, I offer my heartfelt thanks to Robert Perron and Euigoo Kang for their beautiful English translation of these poems.

Part 1 You and I are

You and I are

1.

Whenever I see glue in a tube
I want to stick to you
Even if you are alone
Even if you are very far away

I yearn to run a thousand li* and become one.

2.

Whenever I look upon Chimabawi**
I want to hang my skirt upon it
To let it flutter
Thereon
I want fluffy clouds to hang upon it
Floating as on feathers
I want to go to you.

---

* Li or ri is a traditional unit of distance. One Korean li is about 400 meters.

** Chimabawi (Skirt Rock) is the name of a cliff on Inwangsan in Seoul. The story of Chimabawi goes back to 1506 when Jungjong and his wife were installed as the 11th King and Queen of the Joseon Dynasty. Soon after, the Queen was forced out and moved to a village near Inwangsan. Heartbroken, everyday, the King would go to a vantage point in the palace and gaze toward his wife's village. Upon learning this, the ex-Queen hung her red hanbok skirt on the cliff.

The Cornelian Cherry

Unfurling its yellow wings
Soaring with ease
To catch a sip of sunlight

The flower that becomes a butterfly
Takes pity on the sunlight
And caresses it with a yellow hue.

The Wall

I sit and face the wall
That stands in silence
That could not be broken down
It resembles the silence of my father
With a heavy burden on his back
I close my eyes.

The Cosmos

Between the lapels of a jeogori[*] tunic
Flutter her petals

Tumbling through the sky above
Coming closer on the wind

Sad hard times, she writes
The type rolls off her fingertips

As a shooting star falls to its demise
Her eyes lighten.

---

[*] *The jeogori is the upper part of the hanbok, a traditional Korean garment.*

The Joy of Being One

Pushing hard, a leaf emerges
And finally blossoms into a flower

You always wanted
To open the closed keyhole
Between our two countries
I'm glad that we share the same abode

I see the husband as the honest land
The wife as a flower
The angel of our home

Breaking bread together
Becoming rich with faith, hope, and laughter
Watching the sun and moon
With the aroma of strong coffee
Wishing every morning
By a flowering window, always a pair
To live like singing birds

Life

You sail on a distant sea
You thirst under a burning sun
The storm
Shakes your boat

If you hold hands
Singing words of love
Deeply etched in your hearts
You will navigate the rough seas
Through blinding wind and rain

Follow the path of the seagull
Do not fear the journey ahead
But reflect on its days
Let it be a guiding light for others

On a voyage you dare not take on your own
If you travel together
Even in strong storms
You will reach the island of tranquility
Where green forests await you.

The Resurrection Lily*

Longing for him dearly
Longing for an impossible relationship
Your blood red heart
A clump of resurrection lilies

The unfulfilled love of a lifetime
Rises from the ashes
And shows him your burning red lips
Your dear love

Green pine twigs on the fence
Long for his coming today
Your doleful flower decorations
Long that his breath
Arrives on the wind

Your deep yearning
Shakes the bare flower stalks
Wanting to be hugged by the wind.

---

* *The Resurrection Lily is a herbaceous plant with basal, simple leaves. The leaves sprout and grow in the spring, then die during June; flowers appear in late July or early August. In Korea, it is known as Sangsawha (Lovesick Flower), as the flowers and leaves cannot see each other.*

Nelson Bay* Beach

Looking out on Nelson Bay Beach at daybreak
For those who lost hope in life's darkness
The sun, burning its flesh to illuminate the world
Dazzles the flesh of the beach
With glimmers of gold and silver hope.

The morning clouds on the horizon
Unfurl a canvas of my hometown in Chungcheongbukdo
Telling me to send to the village people beyond the mountain
An armful of my warm love, floating on a tempest
Alive and dancing, the sea prancing to Arirang
A nostalgic screen surrounds the white sand
To subtly reveal my homeland.

The smell of salt and fish wafts through the crashing surf
A double long hanbok flutters to the lilt of a bamboo flute
Backlit in dark orange like a dancing clown.
Even if pain approaches like a flock of seagulls
I want to send my unspoken words
In a missive to the East.

Longings that I could not let go of for a lifetime
The crashing sea brushes over a foaming rock

A Hibiscus syriacus** blooms in its place.

---

* Nelson Bay is a resort town 150 km north of Sydney, Australia.

** Hibiscus syriacus is a species of flowering plant in the mallow family. Common names include the Rose of Sharon, Rose Mallow, among others. It is the national flower of South Korea.

The Sorrow of the Pearly Blue* Plum Blossoms

Crystal beads hang in white sorrow
On the buds of the blue plum blossoms
The plum lady stares at the clouds

She hangs her endless suffering on the blue mountains
But drapes the bridal veil that hangs around the peak
About herself and lives her dream

Perched on a thin branch
The bush warbler coos sad songs in the morning
The plum lady sheds quiet tears
For the flowers that floated away in the monsoon rains.

---

* *A blue plum blossom has white petals and greenish stamen that gives the impression of a green flower, despite its name in the Korean language.*

Camellia Girl

In frigid wind, the red bud bites the white snow
As years pass, watching the flowers in full bloom
The child's face blushes
Like the morning sun that throbs her heart

You are the lover holding flowers at the Dragon Gate
Concealed for a long time
You try to bring forth fresh feelings
The moment you missed him
You kept your dark red feelings to yourself
Now those camellias are in full bloom
Even after many years
Lips pressed for the first time still feel hot
And you recall the flowers stolen from you

Heaven and earth create many patterns
The verdant camellias bloom and fade
The red bud mulls the times gone by
And melts in the white snow.

The Wisdom of Spring

Flowers also have wings
Petals longing to hug the land after its winter freeze
Spread their wings on a spring day
Covering the land with downy hair

Even if piled and trampled on, flowers embrace the land
And give thanks to the heart of their rooted life
When the sunlight ripens their faces
Flowers thank the earth for letting them rest

Sometimes flowers spread their wings to push away
The rain and wind that shake and wake them
They fall round and round in illness
Fending off the rain and wind

Dizzy, the raindrops and wind sit on thin branches
Blowing kisses and poking fun at the flowers
The hearts of the flowers churn like the ocean
Yet the throbbing hearts do not hate the wind
But embrace the earth for the next life
Brought by the rain and wind.

As Time Goes By

On a day I miss my dear loves
I want to sear your memories
In the sunset on the river

Like burning red petals
The river shimmers
Embracing even my heartfelt sobs
And swallowing them in its quiet flow
On a day I miss you most, the wind is calling
I want to cry like a running stream

In the warm sun, the autumn leaves fall
As they flow with the river, I think of my dear loves
I want to let my heart flow
In the direction of the falling leaves

By the side of the river in sunset
O those I miss, those I miss
The tales of flowers I cherish with broken heart
I want to let the yearning flow without abatement.

Beholding the Magnolia

The white bells toll.
Their sound in the wind
A low alto.
Drunk on the night dew
The alto bells stagger.
The sound of music spreads on the wind
Boasting beautiful wings
A pair of mandarin ducks soar up into the sky.
Firecrackers explode
Welcoming the May bride.
Guests too are boisterous.
Wearing white flowered shoes
The bride follows their scent.
Look,
A candle in the midst of that white resonance.

The Evening Primrose

A fragment of moonlight
Peeps from behind the clouds

Yellow chicks
With a slip of a smile

Hiding petals during the day
Dreaming of distant clouds

The dewy flowers
Await the moonlight to bloom

Long necks sway in the wind
The flowers shed tears

The Black Locust

When I think of playing elastics[*]
Wearing black rubber shoes
I suddenly smell black locust flowers.

At night with black lips from kkambugi[**]
Snug like a mother
Squirrels, rabbits, deer
Look for a place to rest,
The black locust flower in my heart
The kingdom of night whispers.

In April
Grandmother made us black locust flower fritters
I bathe in the fragrance of black locust flowers
Emerging white even in the dark of night.

Flowers silently open their eyes
Birds are chirping
And the childhood night of the black locust fades away.

---

[*] *Elastics or rubber band games are children's games resembling hopscotch and jump rope.*

[**] *Kkambugi is the blackened head of barley or wheat. Children in rural Korea used to pick this up and eat it, smudging their lips and tongues.*

The Rose

I build a flower garden in my heart
The fragrance waves at me

In the house of roses
The bipa-playing* queen lives in stamens

In the house of roses
There glint the swords of soldiers
Who toil to guard the queen

For the soldiers who will return
I build a palace of roses in my heart.

The bipa is a string musical instrument that has a pear-shaped wooden body with a varying number of frets. It has either four or five strings. This lute-like instrument is played by plucking the strings.

An Apple

She wants to resemble the red sun, her red skin
She wants to embrace the round moon, her round face
A chubby body dropped upon the world after ten months
Sometimes even her heart resembles the forbidden fruit

When a desert-like stillness arrives
She wants to kiss a man
When her red flesh is dug out
She swells with an unending fountain of juice

Under an autumn sun she would be sad no more
He'd take a bite and cherish a distant memory
Now she makes everybody drool
Now she leaves alone with a red glow in her wake.

Inosculation

Between pine needles quivering in the breeze
Stretch branches
To connect your arteries
You open your bodies little by little
You breathe life into each other's passionate soul.

In and out of the twigs
The breezes
Would breathe life into you.

Even after years gone by
Even in the pain of breaking
You would not let go of each other's hands.

In order to care for each other
Going back and forth between past life and this life
You have promised to be one.

Do trees stretch their arms in yearning?

A Sinking Day

On board the boat of time
A rose peeps into the window

Her ragged breathing is so hot
It could burn the night

The sky stands like a blue saint
To sow the seeds of hope
Will the pilgrim embark on a journey

Will she leave smudges of wine on her lips
Will she have to wipe away tears a little too

Even as time goes by
It tickles her with memories.

The Sound of Crickets

Inside me a bright red apple
Hangs
Like a train heading for the last station
It has a destination

During my long journey
Insanely, secretly
To the one hidden
Through the dark night of whirring crickets
I want to whisper

Like moonlight slightly obscured by twigs
Flows on a river
I want to find your window
And sing a cricket's song.

Palm Beach[*]

Along the scatter of a red sunset
The sky tenderly meets the ocean

The boat of eyebrows you row
Stows a yearning at the end of the horizon

When a cumulus cloud
Rises above the horizon
Buzzing like a party house
The beach at twilight emerges

Was it one day in August?
I sent a message in an empty bottle
To a soul
At a port that belongs to no one.

---

[*] *Palm Beach is a suburb in the Northern Beaches region of Sydney, in the state of New South Wales, Australia.*

Mardi Gras Festival

Bonjour Mademoiselle
I would like to buy a pink dress
Would a purple hat go well with it
Oh, I need a long wig too
What about a strawberry lipstick to turn my lips hot
The sunlit streets may lack fragrance
But are sweet as strawberries at night

On the streets of Feb, we'll be teddy bears with lollipops
We will sing while sipping lemon Oskis
In front of a parade of flower cars we will buzz like bees
And croon cheerful songs
Bonjour Mademoiselle bonjour Michelle

When your sweet and sour lips are touched
Your ruddy face
Dazzles like the fireworks of Mardi Gras
The heart on your tiara flashes
Have the fireworks become butterflies and flown upon it

Infatuated with
Drone bees and their beauty
Are you buried under their pollen
Through the streets covered with fragrances
You are about to start a pride parade
And sing the songs of love.

Jacarandas

Lose yourself in the fragrance of heavenly jacarandas
Bees buzzing like a man mad for a woman
Buried in a blanket of pollen

Jacaranda gypsy girls
Do their starlit flowers regard the sky
Hanging lanterns and clamoring trumpets?

Star-shaped petals float in the air like butterflies
Purple cancan skirts
Spread on the ground and roll out a regal carpet

For those who pass the flowered lane of your falling pain
Do you feel happy?
A cancan festival on earth
Do you hear the trumpets on every street?

A Possum's * Love

A possum lies lifeless in the road
Waiting for a passing car to crush it
During last night's lightning
In pursuit of love
Climbing the electric wires
His life came to an end

Leaving behind a love story like a passing cloud
Leaving behind a teardrop in her heart

Love oh love although a magnolia in spring
Is a cascade of separations falling over a rock face

A knife presses against the back of life
Like the death of a possum on the road
Scanned by the wheels of passing cars.

---

* *The common brushtail possum is a nocturnal, semi-arboreal marsupial, native to Australia. Around human habitations, common brushtails are inventive and determined foragers with a liking for fruit trees, vegetable gardens, and kitchen raids.*

On the Way to Wagga Wagga[*]

The endless highway
The blue sky
A rainbow fairy adorning the downy flowers

As if it were shy
A telegraph pole standing high to cover the sky
Looks desolate.

Yellow wildflowers on roadside carpets
Giggle as a breeze tickles them.

A herd of spotted golden cattle
Grazes contentedly in the pasture
Petulant clouds pour raindrops
Pressing each other's flesh
Flocks of white sheep enter their pens.

Even if there is darkness, the sun will rise one day
A short downpour of rain, the sun embraces me
The buoyant cows bellow for their mothers
On the way to Wagga Wagga, I see my daughter.

---

[*] *Wagga Wagga is a major regional city in the Riverina region of New South Wales, Australia. It is located 452 kilometers southwest of Sydney.*

A Cocktail of Life

I pour a cocktail into a glass
Money, first love, and honor pour in too

Sweet temptation on the spur of the moment
Can leave you with bitter tastes
Can leave you with sweet tastes
The splendor of the margarita
Glows like a neon light

Looking back at life's journey
I pour my future into the glass

Like the love of my man
I want it to have the refreshing scent of pine
Shaken well
In the gardens of my life
I hope to meet you green and fresh.

The Surf at Manly Beach[*]

The sea loosens a jade skirt
Unfurling its heart on a sandbar.

Rushing foam rolls over the sandbar
Digging into the bodies of lovers.

A twilight sea slightly hidden in dark clouds
Splash, splash, splash! Hot music blares
November youths are riding the waves.

The heads on the boards are distant dots
Waiting for rainbow dreams over the waves.

The sea unfurls a skirt woven with white lace
And rushes onto the sandbar in white droves
Becoming seagulls flying with hope.

---

[*] *Manly is a beach-side suburb of northern Sydney, in the state of New South Wales, Australia. Manly was named by Captain Arthur Phillip for the Indigenous people living there, for their "confident and manly behavior."*

The Jervis Bay Beaches[*]

The blue-eyed Aussies are coming in waves
Running over the white foam
Not jostling, pushing and pulling slowly

With an unlit lighthouse in their midst
They rush in gasping for breath

The secret drawers of the blue-eyed Aussies
Are full of discarded plastic bags, torn clothes, old shoes
And unfurled fishing nets
Why does their skin blister?

The blue-bodied Aussies
Roll endlessly in pain

Like them
With the baggage of my heart tied to a way station
I repeat my life wherever it takes me.

---

[*] *Jervis Bay is a 102-square-kilometer oceanic bay and village about 200 kilometers south of Sydney, on the south coast of New South Wales, Australia.*

The Strathfield Memorial[*]

Arriving at the Strathfield Library
Memorial, I meet the names of Korean War veterans
Swept by wind and drenched in drizzle
The monument shimmers
A five-letter name on a rusty plaque
Shimmers in emerging sunlight

With bloodied legs he knocked on my door
I hid him in the attic of the barn
My grandmother's old tale
Of foreign soldiers with names like
On the Memorial

July 1950, Kapyong[**]. John Davidson and many others
The names of those hugged leaving on their long journey
I think of families and girlfriends
Who received the news of death by telegram

Etched on the Memorial
O brave Aussie warriors!
Not even a mourning light
Now a haven for birds
O brave Aussie warriors of the Memorial!
Do your souls yet reside on the Kapyong streets?

Drizzling today
The names on the Memorial look so forlorn
I stop for a moment to say hello
And brush them with my hands.

A Wanderer's Repose

My heart leans toward the Southern Cross
Why do I drift between two countries
Wandering in the crowd at Gwanghwamun Plaza?

Opposite from the Gwanghwamun Intersection
Stands Sydney upside down
From one end of the earth
I look upside down to Sydney
The clean air rising, the blue sky, the chirps of birds
I miss my children in Sydney.

Whenever I look at a street sign in Seoul
Sydney Tour four nights and five days
Sydney Beer, Sydney Shops, Sydney Shoes
The Seoul evening dazzling in every alley
A scattered Sydney glimmers and glows.

My childhood song went like
Hibiscus, hibiscus, our national flower
Wherever I go I look Korean
I am Australian in Korea, Korean in Australia
Even in Australia the Koreans

Eat doenjang-jjigae* and kimchi
In the 1980s Koreans left their longed-for homeland
In photographs and roamed about
Working day and night all week
Playing golf once a week
Hard and lonely for sure
Out at dawn to work for twenty-five dollars an hour

36

Dressmakers, kitchen hands, laborers, nannies
When it gets hard and tiring, they go to Strathfield Plaza
Korean restaurants, grocery shops, beauty salons
They go there to hear the rainbow lorikeets sing.

Strathfield is
A Korean meeting place like Itaewon
A stage for Korean poets to recite
And a rest area for the elderly
Do the people in Seoul hanging the Sydney signs
Light the night you miss like the immigrants in Australia?
Thirty five-years abroad, when I think of my hometown
Even the cotton belt around mother's waist brings tears.

---

* *Doenjang-jjigae is a Korean traditional stew-type dish, made from the primary ingredient of doenjang (soybean paste).*

Samsara[*]

On the day the rain fell and the wind blew
A kookaburra[*] left its nest in the tree.

The storm that tore the world apart
Unclothed the tree
The sunlight laughed at the havoc nonchalantly.

Shattered lives fallen from the branches
Are driven by the wind into the rocks
Wilting under the sunlight.

The ants and larvae
Tunnel into the rotten tree to build homes.

During my lifetime
Endless storms lashed me
Breaking my branches and leaving scars.

Later, the pieces of broken thoughts wriggled back to life.

"When a rotten branch falls with a thud
Why do kookaburras fly away trilling and laughing?"

In the distance the chirps of birds echo
As if heralding the next life.

---

[*] *Samsara in Buddhism is the cycle of repeated birth, mundane existence and dying again. Samsara is considered to be suffering, and in general unsatisfactory and painful, perpetuated by desire and ignorance, and the resulting karma.*

^{**} *The laughing kookaburra is known as the "bushman's alarm clock" because it has a very loud call, usually performed by a family group at dawn and dusk.*

Poems Hidden in the Snowy Mountains

The snowy mountains tell me to forget about love
To hide the stories behind the clouds of a waning moon
To go just like that to the field when the sun and moon rise

The night my dear love does not yet come for a visit
A bereft turtledove coos sad songs in the winter breeze
My love's past image vividly comes to life

Yearnings stacked in my aching heart
Layers of pain frozen in winter's snowflakes
Every letter of the poem an impossible relationship

My heart is a star and a moon
Far away somewhere in the universe
Marking a white space
A star falls from a blue soju glass

With nuanced words tinged by deep longing
I leave a message of union on Ojakgyo[*] Bridge
Long years of hardship
I want to cover them with impetuous passion

In the pitiful night I endlessly gaze at an empty sky
The cool writing hidden in my heart, where has it gone?
My dear love hides in the street of poetic composition.

---

* *Ojakgyo is the bridge crows and magpies formed over the Milky Way for lovers princess Jiknyeo and herder Gyeonwu who are allowed to meet only once a year on the seventh day of the seventh month, according to a Korean folktale.*

The Black Locust and the Eucalyptus

Branches of gum trees stretch toward the sky. Entwined in their midst is a black locust, as though married to them. Did it give way to the gum trees dominating the sky? The black locust cannot stretch its branches but lives in a tilted posture. The black locust reminds me of myself. In a shaded corner swept by a cold breeze with shadows hanging down, it stands tilted at forty-five degrees.

I now live beholding the space between the red scars of the horizon and the clouds. I sway as the winds blow. Remaining as a trace of those winds, I will love even more the scars of my worm-eaten wounds. And I will be a sturdy black locust that blossoms and bears fruit.

Can I provide sanctuary for squirrels, lesser cuckoos, and bluebirds from the rain and the wind? How much can my long shadow sustain between winter and spring? I want to tinge my heart in the glow of the sunset. Even though my body may soon fall, flowers will bloom on it. Between winter and spring, the sun will cast warm shadows through my branches. Standing aside a little, I will become a deep-rooted tree in the sway of the rain and wind.

At a Hunter Valley Winery

The cellar door at Tyrell's Wines
Seeing a 120-year-old cellar at the winery
I feel like the owner of the winery
Among aged oak barrels under an old tin roof
I pull myself into the time of grapes.

Grapes gleaming in the vineyard
Grapes ripening to gold
The aroma of fermentation
Flowing from stainless steel barrels
Grape juice paralyzes my tongue

Grapes crushed by hand bubble up
The color warmed by a dream deeper and sweeter
A gentle breath into the charred oak barrels yields
An exceptional taste and aroma
The moment my tongue touches
Tipsy with the melting taste and aroma
I am drunk with golden magic.

Even if life twists and bends
Let's all become grapes in the vineyard
And learn to live a joyous life again

Backyard of the winery
Like the life of a 120-year-old Queensland bottle tree
Chardonnay that embraces aged aroma
Lends life a clear and golden splendor.

Part 2 Grandmother's Dream

G'day Mate

I sort and deliver letters, and today I go to the post office through an early morning fog. A blond-haired staff member brings a bundle of letters and registered mail for sorting. Cool air from the letters going into the boxes raises thorns on the back of my hands. My daily work is judged by how fast I put those letters into the boxes. My hands freeze in front of the boxes and refuse to move. By late morning, I manage to finish work and go to school. At over forty years of age, I go to learn those curly characters.

As I enter the hallway, Mr. Albert walks in. He greets me with g'day mate. Out the window, a cloud resembling sweet ice cream covers the sky. Someday I will fly on that cloud too.

To Seoul. To Seoul. G'day mate!

Strathfield

Strathfield has a plaza like Itaewon[*]. A gathering place for Korean groceries and restaurants. Vietnamese Pho restaurants and cafés. Fast food joints and beauty salons. Korean chicken restaurants, dumpling restaurants, and optometrists. Korean-style Chinese restaurants. Behind them, a train dragging the thunder of time rushes out as if opening a path back home.

In the afternoon people of all ages from India, Nepal, Afghanistan, Korea and China congregate in the plaza. As traditional costumes from each country flutter like national flags, an evening glow engulfs the plaza. The rainbow lorikeets nesting in poplar trees form the orchestra of Strathfield Plaza. They send evening greetings to all who pass.

In the plaza, I sometimes see a boy of about fourteen. He holds a roll of kimbap[**] in his left hand and a smartphone in his right. Hiding a choking voice, the boy taps home into his mom's arms. On the edge of the plaza, buses pass. Young international students and migrants squat there with homesick hearts. At the bus stop, I glance at excited lovers kissing and bring up past memories. A woman exuding poems wilting in Sydney, smiling, reminiscing about her younger days. Are you well? As the train rattles, I send him my regards.

---

[*] *Itaewon is the area surrounding Itaewon-dong, Yongsan-gu, Seoul, South Korea.*

[**] *Kimbap is a Korean dish made from cooked rice, vegetables, fish and meats that are rolled in dried sheets of seaweed, and served in bite-sized slices.*

Grandmother's Dream

Whenever I see bed sheets hanging on a clothesline
I think of my grandmother

The starched bed sheets rustled like dry leaves
The day I put away her shoes and cane
The teary white sheet became a wet handkerchief

Always singing "Tear-soaked Tumen River"*
Grandmother dreamed of returning home
Her knuckles thick with wrinkles, her fingers bent
"Dear old brother" she scribbled in child-like writing
Remembering her childhood under the white bed sheet
Playing hide-and-seek

Even with a wiry body of autumn leaves
Grandmother was a girl who kept her childhood dreams
Even if she kept writing about her unreachable hometown
Letters to her older brother that could not be mailed

With teary eyes during her lifetime
Under the white bed sheet
The dream of the North filled her longing

You know my hometown is Pyongyang, North Korea**
Somehow I came down to South Korea
Unless I die I shall return home for sure

Now her dreams hide in cumulus clouds
In that fluttering white bed sheet
Does she come and go freely between North and South?

---

* "Tear-soaked Tumen River" is a Korean gayo (popular song) by the singer Kim Jeonggu in 1938 when Korea was under Japanese occupation. This song is still popular among the older generation.

** In the next three lines, grandmother soliloquizes in a Pyongyang dialect that has a distinctive accent. The northern accents can be musical, although a little combative to the southern ears.

A Fragrant Soap

Touching him in the morning, first
I wish myself calm and clear

His fine thick scent
Moves up and down my body
Hides inside bubbles and floats on the clouds

As the scent of vanilla always blows petals away
I meet his pleasure

Having enjoyed his scent today
Pushing aside a clean heart, a fluttering heart
I leave for work.

The Ivy

The ivy tendrils
Climb over a neighboring fence
And reach out like cats' paws

Whispers in the wind
Trapped in the shadows of the world
Dark and sad light

A fresh light green leaf
From the other side of the fence
Approaches you

Even if we struggle in the wind
We must be good neighbors
Like the cat jumping over our fence.

The Front Loader Washing Machine

Ms Drum rolls her body like a girl twirling a hula hoop
White shirts, underpants and worn pairs of socks
Like raindrops wiping away the dirt of the world

Singing oh la la tra la
Her operator abruptly
Plucks her chest out
Through her round breast, clothes soaked in dirty water
Get tucked in all the way

Her body spins in solitude
Rubbing and bubbling
Cleaning and clearing a dirty life
Turning people's stains
Into white that catches morsels of sunlight

She tidies dirty clothes
With a touch of love
For deeply wounded clothes
She licks them with her tongue

Sometimes clothes reeking of cigarettes
Blur her eyes
Sometimes clothes reeking of alcohol
Make her tipsy
As if drunk herself
She makes a grinding noise
Her operator without mercy
Twists and presses her nipples

A moment of dark despair
Emerges from the raised bubbles
In her body
Many white roses bloom and dazzle
Does pain disappear because life has pain?

My Heart Is a Bolt

A bolt is my heart
Afraid of someone peeking and entering
It fastens tightly

My heart is a bolt
Afraid of someone already inside leaving
It fastens tightly.

Live Octopus

After three years of a widower's life
Mr. Kim went shopping at a fish market

"Look, please, buy a fresh, strong octopus!
Mister, eat this, and you will be hot tonight."

"I'll have to eat it with Madame Jeong down at the rapids.
I'll have to eat a lot with my long legs wriggling."

Brushing back his remaining strands of hair
Mr. Kim slowly dreams of a deep swamp.

A clump of off-season asters lift their heads
In full bloom in the northeasterly wind.

The Tears of Silver Grass

She is shedding a few tears.

The bright morning sun pours down
To drive out the stains of the world
To comb the loose white hair of silver grass.
Who does she want to greet all dressed up?

Cold but charming eyes
Dreaming of being born green grass
Do you want to flush out the stains infused in your heart?

With her long swaying neck leaning on the wind
Even if she tries to get closer to the sunlight
The more she tries, the farther away she gets
She can do nothing but shed a few tears.

The Train Stop in My Hometown

When I was young
I'd go
Where the Forget-Me-Not people live
There stands a train stop named Sillim Station.

Along the ridges of the Taebaek[*] Mountains
The valley where the white snow first falls
Where shabby street trees
Pass by outside the window
A train resembling the tail of a snake
Chugs up the hill of an abandoned mine village.

From afar, the sound of a temple bell floats in the wind
The rumbling train leaves carrying the sound of the bell.

At night in every house
Dried persimmons ripen in the moonlight
In the moonlit three-room thatched cottages
Soaked in the scent of deodeok^{**} wine.

Turning to Yongam-ri from Sillim Station
Bush clovers fill the lane
You can hear the howling wolves complain
Looking up at the poor moon.

Even now
As if grandma is still there to greet me
The old station fills my eyes.

---

* *The Taebaek Mountains are a mountain range that stretches across North Korea and South Korea. They form the main ridge of the Korean peninsula.*

** *Deodeok or lance asiabell,is a flowering plant native to East Asia. The roots of deodeok are used in Korean cuisine. They are eaten both fresh and cooked, or made into wine.*

The Flu

*Nanta***** plays in my head
They beat the muk******
And ring the gongs
Flames of fever spread in the audience
In its excitement, my body follows the beat
My buttocks shake.

Even when I leave the audience
The winter gale that swirls around my neck
The sound of a nickel silver pot scratching the sand
Refuse to let me go.

The calendar spins in a circle
And flutters at my cough
Like the exciting and enthusiastic performance of Nanta
The world spins around.

An uninvited guest from the band that beats inside me
A trail opens in my head.

---

* *Nanta is a South Korean non-verbal comedy show that incorporates traditional samul nori rhythm which in this case is performed with improvised instruments, such as cutting boards, water canisters and kitchen knives.*

** *Muk (or mook) is a Korean food made from grains, beans, or nut starch such as buckwheat, acorns, and has a jelly-like consistency.*

Scanning the River

The flowing mass is heavy
It flows and flows, its undried layers rolling in waves
Breaching even the passage of time
The pregnant light of a moon in full term
Flows like prey fish, bumping and rubbing each other
The river caresses and pats even the passing rocks

Does the flowing mean that the fish
In the river have second hands on their fins?

The river keeps time to my heartbeat
Biting its sway, a fishing rod of time
On days when you need a break, cut a hole in the ice
And pull the bait up in a straight line
Fish are caught on sunlit hooks

Sometimes the river becomes
A sanctuary for frolicking migratory birds
A passage home for salmon nibbling at their longing
Does this rainbow harbor a Dragon King who floats death?

Labor Market

At three in the morning, a frigid wind pierces his nape.
A man drags his crumpled army boots
He sways in the fog.
Wearing black dungarees, hands dug in and shivering
He rushes to the day labor market.
Passing by a food stall, he drinks half a bottle of soju
Trying to warm his frozen body.

Tilting, he peeks among the men who might call his name.
Today, he got a job at a building site.
Those who were not on the list,
Sigh deeply and look at the sky.

They gave up on work today.
Might as well lay out a straw mat

And play a game of Go-Stop* with the cheats.
In the afternoon, the man called out for a job returned.
He grumbled that the money was not great.
(Oh my goodness! What the hell, I feel like shit, ha! So pissed off I can't
stand it! Ah well!)
The man picked up a butt and blew out smoke.

They set a bonfire in a drum on the street.
A cold bottle of soju and a dried squid
Looks like today's dinner.
Tongues are tingling.
Nearby a hot hangover soup restaurant.
The man thinks of his near-term wife and elderly parents.
Yesterday's three-billion won lotto ticket misfired again.
Tomorrow at dawn, the labor market will be foggy. Again.

---

* *Go-Stop is a Korean fishing card game played with a hwatu deck. Typically there are two or three players.*

Choon-ja's Dabang[*]

At the three-way junction in a hamlet, there's a cozy dabang
The delightful old people babbling like boiling coffee
No bad manners, a friendly Chungchungdo "How are y'all"
With their hands coming out of their pockets.

Poems on art paper on the wall
Kim Satgat[**] may take his straw shoes off and pop out.

For half a day in summer fans whir and flies buzz
Choon-ja still awaits patrons on credit.
Egg in a savory coffee mix, morning coffee is delivered
The village head, more important than the President, comes
She plays the TV on the wall for World Cup soccer matches
Watermelon, yellow melon, and dried munchies
The dabang is generous with drinks and food for patrons
Village generosity springs up like the sunrise

Deep endearments like Jangajji[***] run into the mobile phones
The sound of rain merges with the clinks of playing go
A distant nostalgia smolders in red
From the old speakers by the window
Na Hoon-a lyrics "Cosmos is blooming" play
At this country dabang, lovely Choon-ja's skirt
Collects dewdrops from "The Hometown Station."

Laughter blooms to the scent of pines
The flowing moonlight stops and time is tied up
Choon-ja's dabang at the three-way junction in Beolgok-myun, Nonsan
On the go table abuzz with a murmur
Delightful old stories go back in time.

---

* A dabang is a Korean establishment that primarily serves coffee, tea, and other non-alcoholic beverages. An old fashioned coffee shop popular until the 1990s.

** Kim Satgat is a 19th century Choson poet. A vagabond poet, he is famous for his acerbic satire and for wearing a bamboo hat called a satgat most of his life.

*** Jangajji or pickled vegetables is a type of side dish. It is made by pickling vegetables in soy sauce, bean or chili paste sauce.

63

The SNS Watcher

My name replaced last year is NM153501.
Through the rectangle the tap tap tap lights up the world
I look at her head through my eye on the monitor
With a confused expression for several days
Not even combing her hair
Not sure how busy she is in her world
Her metal framed glasses reflected in the monitor
She has long forgotten her beauty as a woman.

Her name is Kang Danbee, age 28
She designs graphic advertising text and colors.
Since her partner a few days ago
Dated a new employee
She has only been writing complaints to me.
But what perfume she wears each morning
Her odor levels cannot be stored in my body.
As a work laptop, I know
Her heart-broken state of mind.

Her mental state is unstable.
I send a red signal to her.
She will soon tender her resignation letter.

I notice she has disappeared through the office window.
Even though I can no longer exchange information with her
Her DNA remains all over my body.
"Someone from somewhere is always watching you."

About the Change of Inflection

Between summer and autumn the type in the diary bends
The woman
Planted a seed of yearning on a page

Read between the lines
There she dampens her despair and anguish
The woman walks the walk of a dinosaur

Her matured back hangs yellow and red
After that summer, her eyes deepened

Someday
The green branches will fly with the birds in the wind
A low sun colors the autumn mountains with a dim light
Flowing and passing with bumpy twists and turns
Because of the inflection, you learn and go forward.

The Chain of Time

We are swimming through time

A burdened camel forced to walk on the sand
Looking forward to an invisible oasis
The weary camel caught in a mirage
Thinks of a lion running swiftly

The lion becomes a child
With the scent of innocence
Clear beads of dew cover the fragrance

How deep is the heart of the dew
If you want to be a child you have to listen to the child
If you want to be dew you have to roll upon leaves

The child doesn't see only what the child sees
The child can see the downfall of God

Don't stand before God in the chain of time
Thinking about how you came to this earth
Cross the borders of darkness for a long rough walk
Find Jupiter to prophesy the beginning and the end.

The Back

Can I live without leaning my back to the world?
Even the wisteria trunk climbs against a pole

As a child, you warmly carried and comforted me
I forgot about the back
Even in warmth, I hungered for love

Even the morning sun leans against a lattice
The foolishness of not knowing that it shines brightly

The spike I drove into
Father's back
Left numerous holes

The shovel of my heart just kept digging hollows
My bent existence, I can't even wash it off with water
I didn't know father's life would turn to a handful of ashes
Once again, I want to remain a fossil on that back.

Self-Portrait on a Black Night

1.

Do the stars see the pupils of my eyes shine
From there stars see my blinking eyes as two of them
My two pupils become stars
Do they know why I send them signals

The movement of the stars is suspicious
My eyes are also dyed black in the night sky
The stars twinkle in the direction I shine
Shooting their light in my round face
My face must look like the moon to them

2.

Do the stars have a language of light
The path of such shining stars
Draws a line at the top of a pyramid
Follow that line and you will reach a fresh stream
Open the door to the stream and listen
It'll be a song of compassion for me
Will the stars see my eyes as stars
And see my face as a circle of light reflected in the mirror

3.
Tonight in the starlit mirror
I saw my mom
Glittering, I heard my mom call me
Her lips which were like garden balsam
Resembled the waist of a star shining very brightly
Anguish on a dark damp day, dew on the leaf tips
Growing into a great star of a woman
It was the glitter of my mom's eyes that watched.

At The Dead Sea

Numerous white crystals sleep 430 meters below sea level
Stone marbles in beach sand spit white blood as if knifed
Who has left so many white shards here?

Lot's wife remains as a pillar of salt
She'd want to turn to the sea and break the salt
My foot boils at 43 degrees Celsius
The sun shines on fragmented sand
Creaking and grinding its teeth

My floating body can't touch the salt floor
A blue waterbed
I am light as a petal
I fear my eyes may be marinated

Under bouncing sunlight, the crystals' salty taste is deeper
I carefully whisk my entangled blue wings
Blue lanterns painted with dazzling crystals float away

I didn't realize standing, lying down the sky is closer
With open eyes you can see the whole sky but not the sun
Across the salt sea, Jordan is visible. They say
While water flows from the Jordan River to the Dead Sea
A Jew crossing to Jordan would become a sheepskin.

The Blades of Caesarea

Crossed the stone bridge at Caesarea Maritima
A flurry of the ancient soldiers' horseshoes
Patterns engraved on columns are Roman clocks

The desert lion opens its hungry mouth
Only the sharp-toothed pillars left by Caesar
The dry sun bites

Between rays of sunlight, a bipa chirps
The sound floats in its rhythm
And crumbles among olive leaves once lush
The only thing not crumbled is seawater not dried up
It pushes and turns so as not to crumble any more
Are there still horses
Marching in the arena pulling chariots

A small gap is visible between the walls
Traces of water runoff in the round channel that remains
Olive groves form a forest of shadows over Rome

The eagle flies, looking over the whole of the Roman forest
I see Rome from an olive tree

It's a stupid channel
The ruts of chariot wheels remain as tattoos
Only blades of swords broken in half remain, rusting
A tree trimmed with a blade remains green even after a thousand years.

If I Stretched Out the Earth on a Single Sheet

If I stretched out the round revolving earth
The sea and mountains would become flat amoebae
Could I put the squishy object in my pocket

In summer, the sound of cicadas
Would be trapped in darkness and not heard
In fall, yellow and red leaves send only starlight signals
In winter, Antarctica would slip out of my pocket
And fold towards the desert

What would people see from the tops of their buildings
Could animals run on a flat earth
When it rains on a flat earth
Where would Niagara Falls flow to

I want to rest the earth's sore back
I want to lay flat the feverish earth
Like the earth, I'm getting hotter

So where am I supposed to stand?

The Red Gap

There are wind paths among the trees.
They are swaying so as not to face each other.

A bird singing on a twig
Trying not to fall
Nimbly flaps its wings and sets its direction.

From the twigs where the bird's warmth passed
Comfortably, the buds raise their heads
Pretending to be shy.

The sun cuts the wind with a red blade
And sprinkles a fragrance in the gap.
Everything comes back.
Tick-tock, the minute and second hands move to the right
To open a path for the swaying wind.
The scent spreads.
The gap between you and me among the trees
Grows with a fragrance that even the wind cannot cut.

Day and night, flowers bloom and fall among people
Their paths to happiness and unhappiness
Curve through the red gap.

His Whistling

His whistling even
Let the moonlight hidden in the clouds shine
Every time he poo-weet
The sound was of clear water falling into a glass bottle

His closed lips broke the silence
The whistling smelt of deep darkness
Even the stars bloomed in heaven and earth

The sound that arrived slowly pushing the wind
Was a broken guitar string
I can no longer hear his trot-beat tunes
The man leaning against a tree and whistling
All that remain on the tree are white chrysanthemums

I miss that sound when I step in the moonlight
The whistling is the sound of a faraway train
The fluttering of a butterfly getting closer then disappearing
His whistling became the melody of a perfume.

The Tree to a Saw Blade

The branch bites a saw blade
Bracing its grains of white flesh before being cut to pieces
It doesn't shy away from the approaching sharp blade

Even though there were days when it fell
New shoots sprout from the trimmed tree
Because there is pain the branch
Raises its own nib and embraces
Its lacerated flesh with the wind

The birds shaking water drops sit on the cut branch
Nursing the wounds with feathers

Even though cut off by his boss on a spring day
He firmly bit the saw blade
Now he pushes the saw blade away
At the end of the cut tree
Let the flower buds bloom brightly.

The Stars' Desks

Looking up at the dark sky
The stars are chained to their desks writing poems

They write on the rocks in deep trails
They write even in the dark of spreading ink wash

Sitting quietly on leaves among the night dew
They embroider poetic words with starlight

Pine trees rooted in stone pillars
The cries of mother deer
Reciting poetry with the starlight

Tiger moths among the streetlights
In the starlight-written verses
Dance

As the stars finish writing and fall asleep
A woman who could not sleep sat by the window
Missing the lyrics the stars sang, she looks for the stars.

Let's Go Star Picking on Sand Island

1.

Laklanta Desert 333. Where the Southern Cross rises, I wanted to see a special star with you. When the sandstorm needled my skin and the red sunset colored the world, we were lying together.

2.

A map of the stars spread out on a wild open plain. Like a rose that never fades, a bear that doesn't disappear, a crown that doesn't fit on the head, like the old clothes your grandmother made, the stars stuck on your body. When new stars are born from the wombs of existing stars, I've seen it through a telescope. I shed tears over the blue light like watching a sad movie.

3.

In the night desert, the stars are sending me texts salted in the wind. I want to find out the street number there. The stars will be a distant guide to me with their movements. We drank together on that road. There was the cracking sound of a star breaking from the glass. I want to be a very bright star. Aboriginal Australians at eighteen walk all night to their coming-of-age ceremony. When a man finds a big star, he builds a sand island and greets his bride like a star. Just as those stars fall, becoming red and yellow meteors on the ground, I wonder if you went there to pick a star.

Mr. Thief Comes for a Visit

Did he jump over the railing, his scattered footprints
Trampling the flower bed, the petals scattered
Even the bright moonlight hid in the clouds

Beneath that blurry wall
The footprints of time are clear
The years of his solo wall jumping
Are stacked in thick layers

Mr. Thief, Mr. Thief
A stray cat gliding swiftly over walls
The sun on the western mountains spreads darkness
And crosses the ridge
Please, steal those hands of time and go away.

The Festival for Peace

Flowers gathered at the Pyeongchang Olympic Festival.
The peonies worried about pollution and were heartbroken,
The cherry blossoms, due to Hiroshima and the tsunami
Even after many years, bled in pain.

Then
The hibiscuses with another heartbroken child inside them
Evoked the story of comfort women, now grandmothers,
And the story of evacuations during the Korean War.

All the flowers lived with wounds.
All the flowers had unhealed hearts
Carefully they tried to bring out a feeling of hope.
Although the flowers of Korea, China, and Japan have different
languages and customs, together
They stamped their handprints on the plaster dough.
The fragrance of peace revealed through their etchings.
The poetic winds of Korea, China and Japan held hands, the winds of
hope.
Just in time, the autumn sunlight ripens the crops in the field to gold
Blessing the poets' songs of peace.

The Vase Behind My Back

While the stars sleep
A gaze from behind my back hurts
I turn my head
A red flower in a vase
Its neck drooping.

A heartbreaking farewell to life
The petal that fell on the floor smarts
The heart of a relationship
Like my mother's life.

Looking intently at only one man
As a man's wife
Agitated for so long
Such was the time she lived
Reflected in the crescent moonlight of the window
A rose is wet with dew
A quiet night, I look alone at the flowers
My mother who lived only for my father
I remember a life lived utterly alone.

The Navel

While eating a navel melon
I look at my belly button and it looks like Tolstoy's face

Grandma's hand caressed me when I was young
As pain cried out from my belly button

Even though my grandmother passed away
Her warm love remains a blooming hot flower inside me
Does her touch from those days kindle in the other world

Occasionally when I see my once upset stomach while stroking my ugly
Tolstoy
The wormwood scent of my grandmother's warmth spreads
The scent, in layers of sadness and longing
Doesn't disappear from the storehouse of memories.

God Is Dead

Praying every day to become an angel
Icarus's wings melt in the sun and he no longer flies
A young life survived in the ashes of Nepal
With a long string around his waist, he climbs
A Himalayan trail with water buckets on his shoulder

The village has long been in ruins
In the dark where not even the sound of rain can be heard
Skeletons lying under the rubble, backs on the ground
Can't keep their mouths closed for wanting to bite the sun

Red crosses on every street of the world
Swallow the entire night
Children wander through the desolate rocky hills
On the carriage no bells ring all day
Skulls pile up and rise to a tower

The carriage in which no donkey brays
What does the Nepalese boy think?
Does the gong ring out from his heart too?

Farewell to Covid-19

Air lanes covered with bat wings
I resent the planes flying out
I miss seeing my family at the airport

If you don't wear a mask in malls and public places
When will there not be two-hundred-dollar fines?
I want to see the white teeth of my laughing friend
No more tapping with the back of your hand or arm
I want to hug my older and younger friends warmly

Who are you with an invisible, horrendous appearance?
In the metro, people babble, faces covered like criminals
Sydney's seasons change five times
On the day the flowers bloomed and withered in pain
A nursing home couple held hands
And uttered just the words "We've been happy"
The husband passed, and the wife left the world a day later
Show your face, you flapping wings of the pandemic!
Schools forgo opening, giving lessons on Zoom instead
When you were not here
We held literary events and birthday parties freely.

People who kept their distance,
With love blossoming in red, holding hands
Want to walk freely in the streets of a spring day
When flowers blow in the air
They want to go on a family trip to historic sites too
We await the lifesaving vaccines to erase you, wicked one.

The Thorny Path of an Unknown Poet

A jing[*] rings in her heart
A life-ending cry
She takes the path of regret
She is a deer, pitiful, lonely and sad

The deer takes a thorny path, a cactus path
A thornbush stings her feet

Wiping her blood-soaked feet
A journey towards a faraway place
May she attain enlightenment
May there be light of life

Even on days of rain and wind
Let the deer wear
A crown of fragrant poetry
On her journey
May there be no black clouds befalling
May there be light of hope

A new world opened by a ballpoint pen
May everyone bless her.

---

[*] *The jing is a large gong used in traditional Korean music to keep beat. It is usually made from high-quality brass and is struck by a stick that is layered with cloth at one end to soften the texture of the sound produced.*

The Daegeum[*]

The sound of playing the stars and playing the moon
Blood flowing in the heart
Dripping like petals
Every time the tune peaks
Thin leaves scattered by the wind
I want to flow to the man's melody

The flowing timbres
Absorb my soul
Soaked in the dark night dew
I can neither come nor go
Sounding like it will break at any moment
I sway with the continuing melody

As if caressing me with ten fingers
The embouchure and finger holes render mournful melody
If I could be one with the tones
I want to be the five senses at the tip of his tongue

O, man playing the daegeum!
Inside your soul
I want to live with a mournful melody.

---

[*] *The daegeum is a large bamboo flute, a transverse flute used in traditional Korean music. It has a buzzing membrane that gives it a special timbre. It is used in court, aristocratic, and folk music, as well as in contemporary classical music, popular music, and film scores.*

Part 3 The Buddhist Temple Bell and the Magpies

The Buddhist Temple Bell and the Magpies

Waking up the dawn
Is not just the sound of the temple bell.

Chatter chatter! Magpies singing in the morning
To spend the day far away
The temperament of time, I once thought
Chatter chatter! Magpies sending forth echoes
To sweep away the darkness of the world
Even the green life lying dormant in the earth
Is lifted up, I feel

When magpies
Open the resting eucalypti's ears
Spreading tense echoes through the air
A curtain of hazy mist rises from the ground
They try their utmost to clear it away with their wings
Like a pinwheel
Beaten by the wind, endlessly spinning
The feathers of the wings follow the wind
Bringing the cool
Driving away the heat of the earth
It's the struggle of time

The chattering echoes cross the borders of the earth
And hang green clocks on the eucalypti
The magpie beaks announcing sunrise and sunset
Will be hard at work, I once felt
Magpies waking up the dawn
Are the Bodhisattvas* of a temple bell

Awakening all sleeping life
The wind created by a thousand hands
Spread out in green fields
When a life pours out joyful cries
Another life stops crying.

---

* *In Buddhism, a bodhisattva is a compassionate being who delays their own enlightenment to help others—all sentient beings—reach enlightenment.*

Dancing in the Air

Early morning, the sound of a moktak*
Ding ding ding, hits the wind
The moonlight, still waking from sleep, in the pond
Gathers its disheveled look
The moktak beats faster, tapping at the wind
The temple candlelight sways
Trying to get through the ahjachang** hinges

Was the previous life of moktak a wind?
The monk's sutra chanting goes over
The mountain peak
And quietly comes back around

Dressed in a gray magoja***
His shaved head bowl-like
That mournful Heart Sutra that crossed the wall
Candle flames shaking their heads
Candle wax shedding tears of karma

At the early morning sounds of a moktak
Woodpeckers answer with peck peck peck
Do they engrave seals on trees to a moktak's beat?
Do they engrave the enlightenment of this world with the Heart Sutra?

The moonlight that saw the scene in secret
Caught the tip of a maple leaf and turned red.

---

* *Moktak is a wooden percussion instrument used by the Buddhist monks that serves to keep the rhythm during sutra chanting. It is an oblong-shaped handheld wooden gong, with a hollow core.*

** *Ahjachang refers to a Korean lattice window. See https://www.pinterest.com.au/pin/693976623804052687/.*

*** *The magoja is a type of long jacket worn with hanbok, the traditional clothing of Korea, and is usually worn on top of the jeogori (short jacket).*

The Winds of Time

Without looking back on the long, long back street
I just ran.
The winds blow for countless hours
Over the mountains, sea, and desert.
The endless sounds of breathing
The repeating dynamics of forte and piano.
In the desert
For a long time, the pyramids
Stand tall.
Even in sandstorms and heat
Standing steadfast
The Golden Ratio of the Pyramid
Who wants to stand against it?

The strong winds and the hot sun
How many billions of eons are they pushing and pulling?
The winds, like the winged staff
Fade a little
Yet not knowing the direction of death
Fly like a kite.
At times, they spread into a storm
At times, they become wet in a rainstorm
Their colored life gets hot then cools
They heat a knife on embers again.

In an instant
Pushing back at the wind to stay alive
Even if the embers are blown out
They look for a new way
To shine a brighter light.

Those are the shoes I threw away
In the place where the flowers faded
Only my footprints remain.
Towards the time when it bloomed blue and red
I walk indefinitely.
Suddenly
Camel's footprints scatter in the wind
Are they heading to the pyramids?

The Wish and the Wind

The wind melts the colors
And carries them in another color
The wind drives the waves, releasing the blue wish
And makes the sun rise low

Evening horizon where the pain of breathing burns red
A wish that new flesh will grow over the red wounds

The unknown lives, young and feeble
Robbed
Now will they flow
Deep into the sea
To sway in billions of winds?

The door of wind and wish
Creaking between the forest and the sea
Suffering from rheumatism between the wind and the wish
The blue and green will
Gradually become dry brown fingerprints

Even if wounds are erased, the wind can't wipe away pain.

Running Through the Landscape of Time

The starry night of Namdaemun, the late market opens
Food stalls opening dim lights
Like mollusks on the move

Hagfish, fresh squid, fritters, japchae*, and skewers
Line up in a single file
A dinner of labor
Through the lights
The blankets of the homeless and cheap sneakers
The midnight scenery at Namdaemun market

Some worlds are closed
Some worlds are open all night
After delivering the night all over the country
A motorbike runs down the alley

Into a jokbal** restaurant, taking darkness with him
In front, a woman begs with a baby on her back
The scene of a few coins

"Get out of the way" hollering down the alleys
The market at midnight rushes a step at a time
Sweat soaked in moonlight runs down every alley.

---

* *Japchae is a savory and slightly sweet dish of stir-fried glass noodles and vegetables, a popular Korean cuisine.*

** *Jokbal is a Korean dish consisting of pig's trotters cooked with soy sauce and spices.*

Clovelly[*] Beach

Are the waves trying to tell you about the world?
Splash, splash, crashing into the cliff
Wanting to tell you about the future
With the cry of a white horse
Hitting the rocks
The horse's mane brushes rapidly
The chest of the clouds
Crashing over rocks
The white horse blurts out a desperate cry
When the white horse rushes in and hits a rock
A flock of birds soars in the clouds
Unfolding a secret story in white

Slam splash! Slam splash!
White foam soldiers scatter
Pushed, swept, and crashed against the rocks
The swing of life swaying by the calls of seagulls
Do they talk of what the floating plastic garbage has inside
Do they fold wings to soothe the rancor of a dead whale
A whale washed up on the sandbar
Under the scorching sun, the gas-filled carcass explodes

The white horse in white clothes
Pushing the violin with a bow
Runs to the rocks to dance the dance of desperate sorrow
Slapping its chest
Slam splash! Slam splash!
Clovelly Beach with seagulls
Bites the bubbles as if trying to endure a painful time

Waves pushing and pulling the world
On the back of a red sunlight
Far away on the horizon
A ship carrying the sun disappears
Pouring out black oil
Rousseau delivers a message.

The Camellia Buds Among the White Snow

At dawn as the white snow fell, my maternal grandmother sighed deeply, coughed, gasped, and passed away. Days after she became a young widow, with the pain of a falling sky and the earth shattering, she gave posthumous birth to an only son in a white blanket, and that night she didn't even bother to light a lantern.

Grandma always carried the things that upset her in her heart. When she was alone, she sang "Lamentable This World" and her smiling face was like a camellia blooming in the white snow. My grandma, who always smoked her cigarette staring at the darkened ceiling, as if burning her fiery bitterness and complaining to her husband in heaven with her white smoke, exhaled "hoooo" and faintly narrowed her eyes.

At dawn on the day she died, I wrote my grandma's name as I stepped on the white snow. As I walked on the snow-covered lane, I saw a figure of my grandma who had made a steaming white rice cake and told me to wait for it to cool down. On the lane, the tire marks of my grandfather's bike reveal its front teeth and eat grandma's white rice cake.

My footprints have not yet been engraved there. A dog came along and followed me, smelling only the old footprints, not mine. On that white dawn of February, the day my grandma passed away without a word, the whole world was blanketed in white snow, covering her life suffered from gossip and hardship in a warm and clean way.

A flock of wild geese guides her path in the moonlight, and in sorrow the wind shakes the roadside trees. The stars fell in droves into my teardrops.

The Sound of the World

1.

I had a long sleep.
I died at the lip of a cliff
Having escaped the world
I can hear clearly how the earth looks and sounds
People who make nuclear weapons for fear of future wars
After the war, by the pond, a lotus blooms inside a skeleton
The shadow of a Vietnamese soul floats in the water.

2.

Peddling seaweed infused with methanol
Knocking victims out and taking their organs to sell
Selling blood during the Cultural Revolution
The People's Republic of China comes into view.

3.

Looking at the moonlit sky
A sleepless night
Wearing ripped shoes
Sticking flyers and picking up waste paper
The man is still hungry.
Having died on the brink of a cliff
I see the light and darkness of the world
Hoping for the day, to see the light of dawn
I see the madness of people praying only for themselves.
When it rains and the wind blows
Earth connected by dots
Threatens life with pollution and global warming.
Even in death, I see things as a soul

Painful news every morning of green roadside trees dying
The sound of flapping birds disappearing
Stone tombs are piling upon my chest.

The Sushi Restaurant

The fishy smell from a frothy sea at dawn
As seagulls tremble
A motorboat anchors at the dock

A live octopus sneaks its feet out of a wooden bowl
Like the Buddha
Carrying the wooden bowl on his shoulder
The owner heads to his sushi restaurant
Foams from a water gun
Beads of droplets collect on the glass of a fishbowl
Fearful abalones on the glass wall
Hagfish and squid seeking long life

Sea breams, mullets, flounders, flatfish with bewildered open mouths
An octopus clings flat to a glass wall asking for help
Shouting out to the world

A Taean[*] sushi restaurant with a shabby crooked sign
Old chairs, stained tables
In a corner, smiling artificial sunflowers covered in dust
A stuffed anglerfish on the wall
Stares frighteningly at me with raised fangs

The owner, on his blood-soaked apron
Wiping his left prosthetic hand
Peels the fish masterfully with his knife
The flesh wriggles even when finely sliced
Staring eyes of fish heads in the corner of the cutting board
Blood and intestines soaked in red resentment

As if chanting Amitabhas[**]
They pout their lips.

The Astilbe

The deep mountain stream
Where the purple flowers bloom

Pregnant with a fawn
A thirsty doe

Drinks and looks at the sky
The place to pee

Hit by a hunter's arrow
On the bloody spot

Those two good eyes
Collect clear dewdrops
Of pink flowers

The Butcher Shop and an OB-GYN Clinic

There is a gynecologist above the butcher shop
Separated by one floor, the doctor's white coat shines

On the day her fiancé left the woman
Through the torn pain
Three months, the redness of a tiny life is assembling

Pushing the bright light away, a young life
Falls into the last swamp and flounders
As if cutting off a side of her flesh with a scalpel
The woman chews the lights from the butcher downstairs

Her ordeal over, she climbs down from the chopping board
And grabs the swaying railing
Hallucinating
She inscribes the haunting cry of her baby on her heart
She hears the growl of the knife from her cut marks

Still, to stay alive she buys a pound of beef
Her torn pain hangs red in the butcher's shop
Like the flesh of a cow.

At the M Bank

A young banker for the stock market talks the talk
Sticking out his pointed chin, he is explaining future wealth

That sharp expression, a pen between his fingers
Showcasing his spinning tricks
He tries to let the client across the table
Sense desired expectations with electromagnetic waves

Scratching the explanations on a piece of paper
The young man's forced smile is clumsy
The knowledge and sales skills in his head
Bounce off like starlight and dazzle

Oh right, you, chicken snout
You're part of the poem I'm imagining!
With a sharp and compressed gaze
With metaphor fragments flying at me as symbols
I'd like to poke your snout
If that would create my fifth book of poems
I would like to buy your product
At a bank, not a bookstore
I want to buy your hardened beak.

The Diet

He and I walk ten thousand paces morning and evening
Constantly paring my belly pear jutting out to the world
My boat of a belly keeps pushing out riding another boat
He and I sit dispirited with those bellies
I grab mine and rub and pinch mercilessly
Imagining the slender waist of an ant

Why don't we eat just for today
He and I stuff food without care into our stomachs
I have to go to a party tomorrow
How am I going to put on a white dress?
Today's resolutions are postponed to tomorrow

Looking at the pretty clothed mannequins in the window
Lit by Halloween lights, as if they were me
I become slim in my dreams
And try on the clothes in the window

Today, he and I are on diets
The flesh not getting skinny but flabby, sloshing like a wave
Even in my dreams, I twirl a hula hoop every day.

Grade School Autumn Art & Poetry Exhibition

Clouds and fog billow over the school gate
Grade school students in yellow and red clothes
Raindrops under autumn umbrellas become a keyboard
Tap tap tap nursery rhymes

Crowns carved on the ground under the eaves
Raindrops fall rat-a-tat-tat to the beat
The art & poetry exhibit in a grade school classroom
Third-graders holding down heads draw red yellow leaves
Soaring into the sky in autumn wind
Hair of rains in straight lines.

Painted with autumn leaves
Yellow and red nursery rhyme on a picture
Like a Picasso masterpiece
Birds fly into the art paper
Autumn poems read by children in blue and yellow clothes
Resounded through the playground
Red and yellow leaves flitter and roll!
The rolling leaves were not fallen leaves after all.

The Crickets and the Vipers

Foam on Palm Beach in falling darkness
As if touching locks of hair loose in space
It smells like the red sea pineapples.

Where the smell spreads

The stars like meongge* slowly reach out to night's palace
Clearing a chaotic world into darkness
The moonlight tickles my lips and pokes my eyes
At that time, the man who left me, left me with a quote
"In the end, enlightenment will come"
The words in my heart hit with the sound of horseshoes

I couldn't read him then
But the dark night swept away with long hair became
A black forest of old symbols stolen billions of years ago
I became an oboe of autumn crickets that roam the night
He became a viper who escaped into the night
And drilled holes through the darkness

When the viper throws its skin off
The sound of crickets that chirped quietly every night
Grows as loud as the waves on Palm Beach.

---

*Meongge is the Korean name for sea pineapple, an edible ascidian (sea squirt) consumed primarily in Korea.

The Yo-Yo

To become steel, it must burn in flames every time
A man is drunk and staggering
In the alley, a panderer grabs his arm
Oh man, we'll treat you great today, a good time huh
He turned around and smiled

Don't call me
At home, I am called money
At work, a workaholic

He drools and staggers
Lashed by waves incessantly pounding the cliffs
A root of his future prospects must have been thinning

Walking around the alley, soaked by the moonlight
He leans on a power pole
Uttering the same drunken words, meets the dawn
A few sleeve buttons disappeared into the fog

The big dream of the young days he longed for
Worn out by the cogs of the world
Became a lost button in a narrow alleyway

"In the world a sin is not a sin if you turn it upside down."

Like the Life of Scott Nearing

Yellow forsythia stand in line
The flower I put on the heads of my childhood friends

Looking at the forsythia hanging on wire netting
I think of the demilitarized zone.

Next to the gun barrels guarding the Bugaksan[*] barracks
The yellow flowers call for peace

It wasn't forsythia watching me then, but yellow freedom
I can see myself among them, always in groups, surviving

Looking at the roadside with the forsythia in full bloom
The days of a heavy heart
Seem to disappear

Spring summer autumn winter
While flowers bloom like soldiers in a joint military exercise
Look back quietly
You can see the trail from shoes crumpled at the heel

Half of my remaining life should be with those flowers
I wish it was a quote from a Scott Nearing autobiography.

---

[*] Bugaksan (342m) is a mountain north of Gyeongbokgung Palace in Seoul, also known as Baegaksan. Inwangsan, Naksan, and Namsan are the mountains that surround the Seoul Basin. The Seoul Fortress was built along the ridges connecting these mountains.

A Poet Couple

When the low-tiled house is covered with white flowers

The scent of black locusts permeates the hanji[*] door
At night, star flowers, moon flowers, and magnolias gather
To paint the backyard white

At dawn, in a small vegetable garden covered with dew
They till the soil and plant greens

In the bedroom, filled with savory Cheonggukjang^{**}
They touch each other's heart and exchange poems

May in Jinbu^{***} is cold and windy with spring rains
When it's cold, by reciting Baek Seok's poems
The poet couple warms the room

An old computer on a small desk
The camellia in the calendar hung on the wall
Drops and colors their hearts red
For the poets who always hid their tears
Hard years flowing into the front stream became poetry
Chirping turtledoves in the nearby mountain became poetry
Poverty growling like a beast became poetry
The silent words touching each other's heart became poetry
Even headwinds all year banging the lattice became poetry.

---

[*] *Hanji is the name of traditional Korean paper, handmade from the inner bark of paper mulberry.*

^{**} *Cheonggukjang is a traditional Korean sauce made from soybeans.*

^{***} *Jinbu is a rural town in Pyeongchang County, South Korea.*

An Unpredictable Cry

Every morning on the eucalyptus branches, a kookaburra responds to the sounds of the heavens, and the blowing wind pushes through the thick air. When the wind blew, the old tree swayed. How the unpredictable, painful sound has become a broken branch! Even the birds in the air folded their wings and waited for a long time.

The landscapes of time in our memories that have passed through lush years are like sandbars lowered by the ebb and flow of the tide. Are the flowers that pass the tree holding the curved staff of the wind? A shooting star from the Southern Cross that chilled the hearts of the flowers falls.

What makes the eyes of an old man who walks his dog daily dampen so sadly? The elderly people go around in a circle; with each step of the way their breath becomes thinner. On a lonely and dark day on Albert Road, on the street of "Jacqueline's Tears," I listen to the endless serenade of farewell.

The people I love disappear one by one into clouds of memories in deep sleep. Luscious life doesn't stay long but goes away with the wind. The kookaburra again announces earthly events to the heavens. Even if a sad gypsy's love fades away, we survive, and sustain to refresh our decaying time.

The Empty Thatched Houses of Hakuba[*]

One hundred fifty centimeters of snow accumulates on each roof of Hakuba. Smells of sulfur in the distance. The Japanese mountain goats follow flocks of crows to the high mountains of Hakuba. When the leading crow sits on a thatched roof over a hundred years old, the mountain goats begin to graze.

The thatched houses do not collapse even when the snow on the roofs makes cracking noises. How many people have stayed here and left! A flock of crows and mountain goats turn their heads towards the mouth of the village, then merge into the evening glow. The mountain goats look at the sunset where the crows fly, and then find a barn with high columns.

In the village, empty thatched houses over a hundred years old are scattered here and there. A bamboo wall fell down helplessly like old clothes. In the yard, the footprints of birds and mountain goats spread out like snowflakes. The mountain goats dream dreams in the house, and chew past hours, led by crows.

In the distance, you can see the stars of Aries, home of the sheep. In the dark, the stars of Aries glance at the mountain goats. At that moment, the mountain goats stare at the sky for a long time burying their footprints, then begin to look for frozen grass in the snow.

White starlight with a tail in its wake flies over the empty thatched house. Under that thatched roof, I become a snowman of the snowy mountains, as in the *Snow Country* of Yasunari Kawabata, then think of my father who left a small mark on this world.

In this empty thatched house that I stayed with a long time ago, the figure of my father shines in the snow as starlight.

---

* *Hakuba is a village in the Japanese Alps, just outside the city of Nagano, which was host of the 1998 Winter Olympics.*

Winter Wind and Window Frost

The bitter wind without benefit of a bow
Flies sharply and strikes
Hitting the window
Digging in sharply between beams of light
Passing through people's lapels and dry leaves

The wind is a rolling ball of shards, slow and fast
Sometimes it rolls through the window
Blooming white flowers of frost
Sometimes it is reborn as a proud Ice Princess
Even if the life of window frost is shortened by the sunlight
It becomes stars drawn by the wind
Stars on the cold glass floor
Shedding tears, pushing the sunlight away

The moonlight melts the darkness and the pale wind
Sweeps with shards and retreats through the alleys
The retreating wind makes a silent protest without arrows
The protest never ends
But hits with a spear of frosty goosebumps
Making every footstep in the alley a stamp
Freezing what remains of a short time

The frozen time in the blink of an eye
Builds a frost kingdom in a once dazzling castle
And spreads wings in the wind swirling for a long journey
As if the wind is not just wind
It discards its clothes and dances on the steaming chimney

Does the wind sing Schubert's Winterreise
As it wants to dance and reach the sky
Rather than stay on the glass wall?
If you listen carefully, you will hear it shhh, whisper
Trembling like a grasshopper in the frost kingdom
The wind wouldn't have been just wind.

The House of a Sydney Woman Exuding Poems

On Albert Road, next to an elementary school where the kookaburras usher in the morning, a Sydney woman exuding poems lives fragrant with poems. With the fragrance, she catches the eucalyptus wind. Elementary school students carrying bags and chatting pass by the front of her garden, laughing like the kookaburras. When school is over, the kids don't leave her house, merry with the fragrance of lush lemon and orange blossoms in her garden. An Indian girl unable to use her legs passes by in a wheelchair. When she sees the girl, like a bluebird with a broken leg, she always feels the life of Stephen Hawking. As if the wind knows it too, when the girl passes by, the chimes by the veranda window sway serenely. The poet is always with children, so she never withers and waits for news from Seoul by the mailbox at Albert Road, Strathfield. Today, the poet who lives at an address in a eucalyptus forest hopes for a world safe from Covid-19 and says HELLO! to passers-by.

That Afternoon

Cream in the sky
Floating darkly
Where does it fly
A sound of rain and thunder
Floating in the air
Unfurled in the clouds
Hiding the sunlight
The dark daylight
Raindrops outside the window
Sad, like tolling a gong.

Port Denison[*]

The moonlight seeps into the blue body. The wind pushes and pulls the blue body. A blue face blows out a cracked, long sigh of white foam. For a long time, standing on the round stone wall, I saw blue eyes deeper than darkness and wider than the world.

The foam rings like bells. The crumbling cries of blue-eyed prisoners, splashing on the stone walls. On a long night, the waves turning a page at a time, the sea breeze makes the sound of a white iron shackle. During the long voyage from England to Fort Jackson, for stealing a slice of bread, the sad breaths of prisoners, who would have fought disease and hunger, came upon me.

The blue sea bleached in the moonlight, prisoners slip the rusty chains into their blue bodies.

At Fort Denison where you can see the Southern Cross in the moonlight, I want to break the chains that bind me.

---

[*] *Fort Denison is a small rocky island in Sydney Harbor, initially called "Rock Island." In the early days of the Australian colonial period, the re-offending prisoners from Britain were sent there for weeks on bread and water in irons. The island came to be known as "Pinchgut." In 1857, the fortress with the battery was completed, and the name was changed to Fort Denison after the then-Governor, William Denison.*

A Neighborhood Meeting at a Cemetery

There is a large and beautiful cemetery on a hill by the seaside. Bondi Beach, adjacent to the city center, is home to unknown birds and wild cats. I like the smell of the sea coming through the darkness. I like walking under the full moonlight. The stars of the Southern Cross fall into the sea, spreading in silver ripples, slap slap, the sound of threshing. The moonlight shines, and there is a strange sound from somewhere.

It was the murmur of a festival in the cemetery. The dead were gathering for a neighborhood meeting. As I listened carefully, they greeted each other, drinking dew and huddling under the dim moonlight.

"Well! Ms. Nancy, what did you do in your other life?"
"I was a world-famous comedian." The ghosts laughed!
"Ok, Michael Skeleton, what did you do?"
"I was a singer."
"You must have been good at singing. Now, the one with a long chin over there, what did John Scarl do?"
"I was in politics in America, then came to Australia."
"Then what did the little Chinese ghost over here do?"
"I did stunts with lions in the circus."
"What did the female Bodhisattva ghost right here do?"
"I swept all the men on the street and made them mine."
"Ah! That sounds like fun." The questioning ghost smiled and winked at the Bodhisattva ghost.
"Right, what did the shy pretty-eyed man ghost sitting in the front do?"
"I was gay. A man like a poppy who gives flowers to every man."

"It must have been a wonderful life. So, bachelor ghost, are you saying that you are also gay?"

"Shh! We'll see each other later."

"Okay, what did the shabby middle-aged woman ghost sitting over there do?"

"I was a real estate scammer. I was a genius at changing the names of other people's land perfectly and selling the land, he he." A male ghost jumped up,

"Hey! Swindler! Because of you, I committed suicide and became the ghost of a well and came to the neighborhood meeting today."

Suddenly, the neighborhood meeting plunged into chaos, then ghosts on horseback appeared,

"What's the fuss? I was a cop. I don't think anyone who is still alive would know that we're having a neighborhood meeting like this at seven o'clock on a full moon night. That the sun sets more beautiful while you are alive, and that there is a third world after death that is more pleasant."

Kim Young-ha, a popular Chatterbox comedian in the 70s, who came to enjoy the beach stroking the moonlight, yelled at the ghosts, "Don't talk!" The ghosts waded through the gloomy and cold fog and slipped into the green grass.

Waves dragging the dim moonlight crashed and splashed, only when it reached nine o'clock, the dead became quiet and the living were like those waves that roared.

The Star Apples

The stars are looking at the apple trees
Their feet melt in the dark
The apples tinted with red

Without the sound of a cry
How can a dawn break
There is only one door to go in and out

Varanasi, India, a partly burned body in the ashes of a pyre
Does one leg want to go back into the womb
The more Bodhisattva sips the Ganges, the thirstier he gets.

The unknowable apparitions
Flow to far, faraway places

Looking for a color that no one has ever found
They take root in the path of a single leaf vein

Stepping into time, then looking out of time
The streets make me dizzy
Whistling slowly, I call a magpie
Among the apple trees
The timbre of a sacred, yet heartless song descends.

Greeting the Night Star

The night that the man who said to be coming didn't come. Only the lips of the waning moon mumble. A shooting star falling from somewhere is like his news. As the stars close their doors one by one and go to bed, I alone watch the waning moonlight. The screams among the hanging eucalyptus branches, the wind must have thought they were a white will and testament.

Suddenly, I think of the story of the tiger and a shaman, and shudder with goosebumps. The story of a shaman who went into a cave to pray, but when she saw a tiger, burned the clothes she was wearing and ran away, then danced to her death. Tonight, as the dead eucalyptus sends greetings to the wind, I am anxious about his news and can't sleep. The cats are mating, and the dog next door is barking at the sky, but I'm alone, crouching like a cowardly tortoise, looking out the window.

The House Move

She packs her household items.
The days that flew like clouds.

Opening her photo albums
Skirts and blouses embrace her slim figure.
As the crouched-in-time moments come out
She envisions her shape returning to her maiden days.

Pages of her memories roll like waves.
Suddenly, in the desert beyond, her maiden clothes find her to their surprise.
Time inflated like a balloon stacks up wearily.

The cactus expands its territory with thorns,
To let its colorful flowers bloom
How many seasons does it have to cross?

Sometimes heartaches move together too.
Her slimmer memories remain unforgettable flashbacks.

Even the days when she was strict to herself
Swept away at times by the move's high and low tides.
Long journeys beyond the window
Time's rattling cart is today's driver and pulls her along.

The Secrets of a Feather

This is a skeleton in a feather
Wings in the wind
My thin shirt balloons and flies

Becoming a light reading of a borrowed poetry book
To be left in a little while
Azaleas blooming on the off-season hills
Even if a hot fire flares for a while
It's a dark secret place
Memories in the forest

Galloping words, hands and palms clapping
As our eyes met, slowly he
Revealed the mystery of a feather
On such a day, the significance disappears easily
Memories of him
A list of the hot fires of hope

When thoughts linger, getting out of control
I walk endlessly, humming songs
It's a feather in a skeleton
An unwritten note, meant to be sent a long time ago.

Yosemite

Sequoia trees stand on the slopes of Yosemite National Park. With bleached dry branches, their whole body burns in the sun. The hanging trees remind me of the old Indigenous Americans who made fires and sang songs. Some trees became tunnels and cars pass through.

The smell of sequoia leaves suggests sad Indigenous American songs. The tree is over 30 meters in circumference and is modest enough, hiding its face at the top of the 80-meter-high trunk.

Suddenly, a black racer snake slithers over the sand. The children scream and try to catch it. I shout, "Please don't catch." The snake may have noticed, as it comes toward me as if asking for salvation. Scared, I step back, but it keeps coming toward me. Not knowing where to go, I hide behind a sequoia tree and hug it. It smells like mother's arms.

The afternoon sun approaches gently. Where the wind blows, a man in an Indigenous American costume sings with a guitar. "If you are desperate to the point of death, come to Yosemite where there are sequoia trees!"

The Kingdom of Night

Baby, sleep
When mom closed the curtains and left my room
The kingdom of night began
My starlight eyes twinkled more
In the thicket in the dark
I called the rabbits out, I called the deer out
I used to run around
At such a time, the moon followed me
Told not to come, the moon
With an unknown smile
Used to light up my back
One day, I escaped the moon and went into a cave
It was full of red and white roses
Tipsy with the smell of roses, I stayed a while then left
The moon waited again at the entrance to the cave
Ah, the boring moon
For my temperature not going down
Mom's magic lamp hung by the window

Now the moon is
Not visible, covered by clouds
In the dark, my tears
Fall like shooting stars
It seems like the moon keeps following me
fling open the curtains to look out.

A Man Raises a Bottle

A man raises a bottle of soju
With his naked upper body as an anju*
He drinks

With red kimchi slices
He throws the soju into his mouth
His heart burns
Just like when he was ill with his first love

A whale pops out
Making waves in his stomach
Like maggots crawling
His memory bores into her body for a long time

I've now become a dried pollack
Tied up with cotton cloth on the hallway ceiling
I am rocking and swaying on a swing
Risen from the ashes with skinny flesh
I am heading back to her.

---

* *Anju is a Korean term for food consumed with alcohol.*

The Soul

A winter leaf says goodbye to the sun
Trying desperately not to fall
Rolling in the wind

The clouds of the sky take their shroud
My father's breath stops, turning into a white pebble
A handful of snowflakes that fell quietly in a heap

My father
Without carrying the heavy burdens of life
In the deeply frozen river
Will his soul
Start quietly all over again?

His urn digs into my hand like the temperature of a lifetime
My father smelled like four o'clock flowers
A roar of his outcry sounded too

His first and last sign of the cross
Who will call his baptismal name Kang Peter?

His soul
Flies like a silver bird on a river
What will it be reborn as?

Nordic Skiing

Nordic skiers run on a white trail in the alpine mountains. Under their feet, the ski bottoms heat up and slide. Cold eyes tie a wind string through the backs of the skiers. The sound of breathing jumps into the air. Ski marks lie like a tattoo on the white snow covering the dry grass. Colorful clothes walk briskly as if they would swallow the whole mountain. The sticky sweat from their bodies melts the frozen forest. At the crossroads of light and darkness, their callused feet dig into the snowy trail. As people aspiring to become the flag of the alpine pass by, snake tails flutter from the ends of their skis. Suddenly, the sound of clouds lifting from the mountain peaks rings out. The ski blades of the leading skier ripped a rock apart.

Part 4 Drinking a Bottle of Red Wine

Metamorphosis

I always carried the key to the safe
Mom and dad called me when they wanted to see the gold

Family members did nothing
But made shopping plans day after day
My father lived hugging a Bentley made in England
My mother was busy shopping for jewelry
My younger sister bought Gucci bags
My younger brother bought Bally shoes and a sports car

Tired, every night
I slept with a black scarf with a white pattern on my neck
I wanted to live far away in the sand of a desert
Maybe because of those thoughts, one day
A poisonous spider started to get tattooed on my back

I, now a redback spider, crawled in bed
My younger sister, disgusted, tried to kill it with F-Killer
Even my parents, looking for me every day, turned away

The light from the window tickled the deadly spider's back
I missed the umbra
Between the quiet and warm shade of trees
I wanted to build a house to shelter me safe as a safe

A place where I can hang in the morning
The redback tattoo in the air, a spider's house
Crossing my feet in the dew that shines like a jewel
I want to make today as precious as the past was painful.

The Mail Carrier in the Woods

1.
Mountain peaks dyed in green
Under a waist of deep misty mountains
A flowing drop of water tickles a blade of grass
As jade beads collecting sunlight thread on the tip of a leaf
Birds peck on the beads
The refreshing sound rolling at the tips of their beaks
Following that sound
On a deserted trail in the woods, the mail carrier comes

2.
You,
Eating the star and moon flowers at the tips of the twigs
Look at Seonnyeobong Peak standing tall in the blue river
A desolate, lonely house where no one comes
Drops of sweat become beads with a green fragrance
He brings you the news
Twelve months of reincarnation, these and those flowers
Under the lonely mountain where bees and butterflies fly
Gazing at the starlight and following the stars
To Capricorn, Taurus, and Cancer
A mysterious alien comes from darkness
After greeting the widowed grandmother
The mail carrier leaves riding the moonlight

Confessions on Saturn

A member of The Aerospace Carrier Expeditionary Force
His name is Gueungbantal based in Washington DC
He has been to outer space several times
The name of the friend he made on Saturn is
Momat Malaku, Saturnian and hermaphrodite
Rather than a long conversation, through their eyes
They feel each other

Forgetting his duty at the Operation Saturn Invasion
Seeing the yellow band floating in the air
Gueungbantal weeps
His irregular heartbeat turns black

In the streets of Saturn only dazzling silver light swirls
Gueungbantal's tears foreshadow a cosmic explosion
NA@M3308's brain tissue can't suppress his job's emotion
The Earth, with several years of time lag, is too far to go

5000 AD
Gueungbantal, a robot that breathes with human emotions
How is he going to deliver his impassioned plea?

A Pizza

The streets of Strathfield race against time
Two fast wheels take the pizza hot
Letting aroma rise at the door

Quietly enduring the fatigue and hunger of the day
Locking the unknown tomorrow in a box
The Combo stuffed with vegetables and meat
Tomato sauce pizza with a bland taste as per order
Shrimp and pineapple pizza set in a yellow circle
The life of stretched mozzarella rolls hot

Unequal banknotes in the part-timer's hands
Even just a single order is acceptable
The youth boiling with hot blood
Runs from day to day
Rings the doorbell and knocks on the door no one answers
A pizza in a box you have to open to see what's inside
The rain slops the floors

A disheveled piece of life
Cut by hand and lift slightly
Stick your warm tongue out
Will a plate of pizza again
Rush on the weary wheels of life.

The Golden Rain

The fall wind is golden rain
I gently touch the golden rain sprayed on the rice plants
And my fingertips tingle with excitement

Whispering merrily in the lush midday
The fall wind dazzles in golden hues
The ears of rice plants in the field
A savory seasoning

Red leaves pour down on the fresh green stalks
Turning them into hot gypsies all too soon
In their procession, the rice plants
Recognize the unique signs of sparrows
Play it safe and lie down in the wide open field

Weeping red tears in the fall wind
The scenery that warms up time
Makes the world bow its head

Drunk in the scenery and soaking my feet in it
In the afternoon when the sunset heats up
My verses too turn to golden rain
Yielding grain at the mill.

The Food Chain

A pond with catfish
Loaches dodging quickly

Not wanting to be eaten without a fight
They do their best to survive, eating vigorously and moving
If the catfish disappeared
It really would be paradise

The struggle to go beyond one's own limits
If there were no danger of being eaten
Would one forget the value and purpose of life?

A mean, catfish-like person at the mouth of town
Who scolded and riled me every day was beaten to death
The monk's words that there was neither good nor evil, right nor wrong

Making life difficult for me and people in the neighborhood
The thug, like a catfish who annoyed and frightened
I didn't know it while he lived there bullying people
That he was a catfish of enlightenment.

Those Days

1.
Railroad tracks passing under a suspension bridge
Women foraging for wild greens

A school of tadpoles in a stream
Their tickling movements
Hiding among the green minari leaves
The sound of beating laundry, thump splat thump!
Splashes its echo into my heart

Country lads thick with ringworm
Press their black rubber shoes in the brook
Almost, but the minnows are as elusive as ever

On the tombstone at big uncle's tomb on the back hill
Laying out food for a playhouse, becoming mom and baby
Making flower pancakes from kudzu and azaleas
Setting the table for jesa[1]
"Aigo[2], Aigo," those wailing days

The beautiful big building
Concerned the stream would swell
Gureumdari Elementary School let us go home early
On summer vacations, collecting insects collecting plants
Teasing, elusive cicadas and red dragonflies
Collecting fireflies in a bottle, playing lightning in the forest

2.
A quiet early evening, sitting on the veranda
Burning dry mugwort to shoo mosquitoes away
We look at the loofahs hanging over the fence.

A game of hwatu[3], of ghosts and goblins
Without knowing, it is late at night
Steamed purple potatoes, sweet potatoes, corn
Their sweetness melting in everyone's mouth
Sip sugar water, eat rice wine lees like grown-ups

The kids ask Gombae[4] grandmother to sing a song
"My hometown is a blooming mountain village"
Clapping hands, they join the singing

At the end of the harvest
The village elders and head of the village pass
We bow to them and say hello

Today, Gaettongi's[5] first birthday

Tomorrow, gosa[6] cakes at freckled Gombo's
The next day, a bull butchered
For Sunja's grandpa's 60th birthday party
Kwaejina-ching-ching-na-ne[7]

Early July, the making of doenjang and gochujang[8]
As the red dragonflies of autumn fly
Large crocks passed down generations
Scouring them to gleam
Warm-hearted chit-chat
Our village suspension bridge

At Chuseok[9], with the rice straw set alight
Full moon, a good harvest, no sickness, no disaster
No legal troubles, no harm but only peace
People in our village pray
In the morning, peanuts and walnuts
Cracking them in the mouth, shouting
Gosurae[10], Gosurae, Gosurae!

3.
Barely a month before down in the village celebrating
The gut[11] of pudakgeori and salpuri, the steaming rice cake
Strewn on the roadside to the beating of music
Magpies the morning guests chirp, chatter!

Several times, every other day
Funeral processions pass the gate of our house
They wail, "Aigo! Aigo!"
Wetting the eyes of passers-by

As grandma says
Our bulldog is jinxed
She bites her nine cubs and kills them.

The pigtail bachelor in our rose garden
His shoveling gets busier
Straw bags and hays go in to make
Winter storage for radish and cabbage
Piled up like a mountain
Chonggak[12] kimchi, dongchimi[13], kimjang[14] kimchi

Then there was no ownership on the hill over the bridge
Would little kids still jump on a board and ride a swing?
Into the night, hearts throb for a colorful New Year's dress
Do they stay awake so their eyebrows don't turn white?

Money pouch full of New Year's bow rewards
Jegichagi[15], ddakjichigi[16], jachigi[17]
Topping, sleigh riding, mischievous kids
The village with suspension bridge of days gone by
Would the dongdongju[18], azalea, and deodeok wines
Still be ripening?

---

[1] *Jesa is a ceremony practiced in Korea, serving as a memorial to the ancestors.*

[2] *Aigo is the word of lamentation uttered by the wailing mourners at the funeral, typically the family or close relatives of the deceased.*

[3] *Hwatu ("battle of flowers") is a style of Korean playing cards.*

[4] *A gombae is someone whose fore and aft head bulges out.*

[5] *A young boy's name that literally means dog shit, named for a happy life.*

[6] *Gosa is a ritual food offering to gods.*

[7] *Kwaejina-ching-ching-na-ne is a Korean folk dance song.*

[8] *Gochujang is a red chili paste popular in Korean cooking.*

[9] *Chuseok is a major harvest festival in Korea.*

[10] *Gosurae is a form of ritual action from Korean folk religion, in which food is thrown into the air after shouting "Gosurae."*

[11] *Gut or goot are the rites performed by Korean shamans.*

[12] *Chonggak kimchi is a kimchi made with a slender white radish.*

[13] *Dongchimi is a type of kimchi in watery brine.*

[14] Kimjang is the traditional kimchi making for the winter.

[15] Jegichagi is an outdoor game of shuttlecock tossing with a foot.

[16] Ddakjichigi is a game of slap-match, played with two tiles of square origami paper.

[17] Jachigi is a stick hitting game played in Korean schoolyards.

[18] Dongdongju is a type of Korean rice beer taken from the top layer of the brewing pot.

The River of Swaying

A small boat is floating away.
I also live life tossing and turning like that boat going alone.
Drinking in loneliness and staggering
Crumpled in the pain of betrayal
I flounder about breaking up with the one I love.
One day when my mom leaves this world
If a boatman can paddle her boat and keep her centered
Even if I sway, unable to ply river winds and heavy rains
I'll be her small boat
Even if it creaks like the arthritis of life
Without torment
I will go without end towards that river shore.

The Moon Is Chatty

The moon brings new news every day. Not the ever-changing fashion dispatch, please, like the new moon, the round moon, and the old moon. I'd like the moon to hug me over my round face.

Shall we cut the moon straight like a watermelon? Open your mouth. That moon looks like a delicious fruit, right? After peeling and cutting, does it smell sweet? Can we smell the sweet aroma of moon fruit in the air?

The full moon shines with a weary light and knocks on the door. If I open the window thinking it wants to eat songpyeon*, it carefully reveals the records from thirty-eight thousand days ago, worrying about the year.

Have you ever seen a moon with such noisy news? It's the moon that knows everything about the world. It seems to solve people's vexed, unsolvable riddles.

I can see the moon always wants to go the way of a quiet observer. Rather, I want it quietly to ride a rocket and hide somewhere in space.

---

* *Songpyeon is a traditional Korean food made of rice powder. It is a type of tteok, small rice cakes, traditionally eaten during Chuseok, the Korean autumn harvest festival.*

The Peony Embroidery

When I sat with grandmother on the warm ondol[*] floor
With the peony-embroidered quilt spread out
To unravel a skein into a ball
The bees and butterflies seemed to fly in

My grandmother told me, still a young child
My life would be like bright moonlight
If I spread fragrances, even on an arduous journey
All would turn out well, like the unraveling of a skein

Pricked by a stinging needle
If we weave flowers like we embroider peonies
Our lives will be butterflies and spread wings of freedom
Unraveling the round skein into a ball with grandmother
Hearing her flower stories
A fond memory of a warm ondol floor I can never forget.

---

[*] *Ondol in Korean traditional architecture is underfloor heating that uses direct heat transfer from wood smoke to heat the underside of a thick masonry floor.*

The Miner

A miner looking for a vein digs the ground
Whether he is digging for gold or digging for soil
His scooping shovel is full of gold dust
The impatient miner hurries his shoveling
He digs deeper and throws everything out
His eyes may see gold
But he can't see gold in his heart
How long does he have to dig deeper

The venting of his anger endangers the mine
Neither miners nor veins are likely to survive

If he cannot see gold even with his eyes open
The gold in his heart with eyes closed is a hundred times better!

The Arrow

Among those who have to block
And those who have to break through
The world puts on wings.

Aiming
At the edge of a never-drying dream
It rolls out time.

Time is an arrow
The green trees say when autumn comes
Pushing against the wind and swaying.

Floating Roses

Are we all roses floating in orbit?
The closer I get, the more the stars push me away.
Wagner and Nietzsche are polar opposites.

The rose seen from the stars
A dot buried in the sand
We are all petals with colors and perfumes
Floating in orbit
Stars remain as shooting stars
Flowers scatter as seeds
Dreaming of a new life.

You and I are roses trying not to wither
Away from a peppery wind
Are we repainting what's gone by?

Looking at the stars to find a big star
Who is trying to make roses bloom?

Father

Look at the rock
It endures heavy rains yet still shows a big heart
Seemingly holding some secret.

As a shelter on the ridge, embracing the salty wind
The rock offers its buttocks
For a long time, looking only at the sky-touching horizon
It wants to fly to a wider world

Sometimes embracing the waves with its whole body
To keep watch for
A day in the lives of moss and cockles
Enduring a breaking body
Settling in one place and enduring frigid weather
Good-naturedly
Keeping its silence, a rock like my father.

The Thrown Umbrella

Listening to a chanson in gloomy weather
Black-winged fox outside my heart
My toes are slipping out
I want to open my umbrella and fly anywhere
Two feet on my head
Two wings on my heart
The black cloud is flying away
Holding the umbrella's tail

Now that even the sunlight buries itself in the ground
Streaks of rain wearing crowns come running with a roar
Under a bow of power lines
The hanging prayer beads of Avalokiteshvara[*]

The garden is far away
Clouds wear black hats and gradually blur my vision
The rain climbs the window like an ivy and sings a chanson
Next to the climbing rain, an achromatic day holds leaves
The leaves only swayed for a moment by the sound of rain

In my spacious apartment, only the sound of breathing
Lightning in the window licks the two hearts of the leaves
Even if it rains forever, if I can drive away my thoughts
I, too, will open my umbrella and fly anywhere.

---

* *Avalokiteshvara in Mahayana Buddhism is widely revered as a central bodhisattva of compassion. His name, meaning "Lord who looks down," reflects his role in responding to the suffering of the world. Avalokiteshvara is often depicted with a thousand arms and eyes, symbolizing his ability to assist all beings.*

The Integrity of Water

Water has bones
Crouching on a cold day
Growing vigorously into white bones under the eaves
It slowly creeps and stretches sharply out.

Focusing the sunlight, from the edge of the roof
It ties the gat* straps and raises frost columns

On a hot sunny day
Where will it fall?
The body melts with a thud
It recoils from the ground and forms a crown

On a warm day, water relaxes to a silky hue
On a cold day, with a vicious and venomous expression
It sharpens its knife and stares at the sun.

---

*A gat is the name of a traditional Korean hat worn by men during the Joseon period. It is made from horsehair with a bamboo frame and is partly transparent, cylindrical with a wide brim.

The Sobs of the River

The river flows, holding back sobs
Can't we just call it a sea of glass?
Where heavy rain has passed
The river flows, burying tears deep in its heart
The sea of glass grieves deeply
At the twinkling light, like hot stabs
But does not announce its existence.

Despite the stinging eye pain
Repelling the sunlight
The river shimmers as a sea of glass
Where years have passed
The story left by
Brothers washed away in heavy rain
Becomes a sea of glass and flows, holding back sobs.

An Unsent letter

George! How deeply were you wronged?
Into that blue sky with clouds and wind
A bird flew freely away

At the age of forty-six, George was without a job
On suspicion of passing a counterfeit $20 bill
Choked by a police officer kneeling on you
You died after pleading for air more than twenty times
Have you left everything in the land where no letters can go now?
Living tears will reverberate in your heart

I thought you had wings a long time ago
I thought you could fly freely now
But still the sound of rain and thunder
I can hear it in the clouds floating in the air
Aren't there just laws there?

Like the day a white bear slapped a black bear
In broad daylight for not giving up a seat
The sound of raindrops outside the window says
Tip tap! knocking on the window and crying sadly

On the street where the white bears play
The black bears weep
From far and near
Their tears started poking and shaking people's insides
Following that cry in the heavens
Lightning struck and thunder roared

We are the red-blooded ones. George!
Living with the same sky, sea, trees, and nature
All I can do is say silent prayers on the other side of the globe
Wishing you repose in the next world
Only wishing that Black and white had the same dignity
I just press my pen on the letter I can't send
To keep it as a record in my diary.

The Sea and the Glass

Drunken sea
Rolling blue body
You sway and I wobble
It's crazy all the same

On the day it stormed, I
Steered a boat and floated to an island
Entered a red food stall on the sandy beach
Swallowed the whole sea with a plate of anago sashimi
That's how I smuggled myself to the outer space of that sunrise

Hey Sea
The wine you sprinkled on the horizon while drinking
I'm going to drink again today
I want to set myself red on fire
To burn it all down
I head for a place where the aroma of alcohol is mellow

In the glass you pour
The salty taste of tequila permeates
Lets me float in the blue sea
Lets me move forward with the power to drive a typhoon

The Life of a Haenyeo[*]

My mama, a haenyeo, drank salty water all her life
Even if, in the depths, she sways to and fro with the wind
Even if she crashes into waves and is cut by a rock
She endured by building a cliff island

Big sister and I stayed on the island and watched mama from afar
Papa was washing windows under the Seoul sky
One day, he flew away from a tall building, becoming a crow

Later a storm hit suddenly
The waves washed my mama away
My sister followed mama
She flew into the waves

On days the waves swell high
Oddly enough, I can hear my sister cry
In the deep sea, seaweed in my sister's hand gestures
Tickles me and pulls me into waves
My body turns to barnacles
Sticking to a rock, I sing songs while waves splash

"Ieodosana ieodosana"[**]
Mother's gone diving, father's gone ashore, no news from him
The splashing waves crash against the rocks, beating my heart...

_____

[*] *Haenyeo are female divers in the Korean province of Jeju.*

[**] *A refrain of a Jeju folk song sung by haenyeos when they dive.*

A Country Beauty Salon

Inside the Muan five-day market is the Park Ho-soon beauty salon. A place that costs only ten thousand won for doing granny's hair. With her late autumn harvest over, granny rushes in. She takes jangajji and kimchi out from the refrigerator and eats it with rice soaked in water, and drinks coffee. It's a beauty salon like a dabang. By the time the stories of the world, the story of a senile grandpa who made a lot of noise during his lifetime, and the bragging of her children blossom to the scent of pumpkin flowers at the hairdresser's table, granny's hair becomes a beehive.

The front yard of a beauty salon where pumpkin leaves turn green on a rainy day. She makes it easy to open the door on the right and on the left so that the grannies can come in comfortably. A beauty salon that giggles even when you call Park Ho-soon Pure Pumpkin*. Open the right side, and you see Park Ho-soon with bubbly perm hair. Open the left side, you see the black dyed hair of Pure Pumpkin.

The day when the grannies with their ramen hair go to see their sons in Seoul. Hairdresser Park Ho-oon gives them a bubble perm under the full moon. The moon hidden in the clouds plays Beethoven's 5th symphony and knocks on the door of the beauty salon. Even if the bee-stinger granny across the road looks at the moon and says, "Wow, what's banging the windows," the bubbly perm moon illuminates amber pumpkins with its golden light.

Park Ho-soon, when read back to front, becomes Soon Ho-park, which means pure pumpkin. It suggests she is not good looking.

Home Alone

The sound of cicadas pierces my ears.

My sighs too are hidden in the sound of the cicadas
The sweltering heat penetrates my skin
The sound of a fan weighing the wind is loud
A fly makes me exercise, breaking my boredom

I watch the news
Stalkers only target women living alone
My heart pounds at the sound of footsteps outside the door
I hear the faint sound of slippers harmonizing with the cicadas

All afternoon
Waiting hangs on the hands of a clock
Only the gas inspector and a delivery man came and went
Loneliness and fear surge
I am now a pine tree on a mountain cliff
Standing alone.

Drinking a Bottle of Red Wine

1.

Seoyoung Anna Kang now lives in Sydney
As a lyricist exuding the fragrance of poems.

She turns the earth backward and rides her time machine
Curious Greetings exchanged on Saturn's Saturday?

How are you doing, Mr. Park Chung-hee?
I was shot down leading the New Village Campaign*
Now getting my daughter to change the history books**.

As she rode a rocket as a robot, Abe Lincoln sat there.
How are you doing?
I liberated the slaves, and Barack Obama is praising me.
Not to mention Michael Jackson is here
To show me how to do the moonwalk.

As she got into the boat, she saw a man floating on the sea. It was
Douglas MacArthur.
How are you doing?
With pipe in mouth, is all okay with the sea off Incheon?

2.

A person cried for spiritual love only and became strange.
How are you doing, Mr. Plato?
Ideally, I am doing well.

How are you doing, Mr. Benjamin Franklin?
I am tingling as if struck by lightning.
With my new invention, I hope it continues to thunder.
As lightning flashes, unable to hear a sound
Beethoven has something to say.
Mr. Franklin, I live with the noise muted.

---

* *The New Village Movement was one of President Park Chung-hee's signature political campaigns to modernize the rural South Korean economy, his main support base.*

** *Park Chung-hee's daughter President Park Geun-hye attempted to change the history textbooks to suit the conservatives' political narrative, but she failed.*

Author Profile

Anna Kang, a Korean Australian poet living in Sydney, has published six books of lyric poems in Korean: *A Secret Garden* (2008), *The Scent of My Mother* (2011), *The Oasis Dries Up* (2014), *Greeting the Night Star* (2018), *The Buddhist Temple Bell and the Magpies* (2022), and *Mozart in My Heart* (2024). Her seventh book is in the works. Her poems in translation appeared in the *ANYDSWPE 2023 Anthology* and the *ANYDSWPE 2024 Anthology*, and *And Then* Volume 22.

Anna is a member of *The Society of Korean Poets*, and is active in other major literary groups in Korea and the Korean diaspora. Anna is a Children's Storyteller in Korean.

Translator Profile

Euigoo Kang lives in Sydney with his wife, Anna, a poet. His love for the outdoors has led him to trek the mountains of Korea, Japan, Australia, and the Himalayas. He spent his career in Information Technology, working in the manufacturing, construction, and banking industries across Korea, the Middle East, and Australia. Prior to that, he served in the ROK Army as an ordnance officer.

He translated *The Blue House Raid*, a novel by Robert Perron (https://robertperron.com), and a series of crowdfunding stories and a photo-essay book about South and North Korea's Baekdu-daegan mountain range by Roger Shepherd (https://www.hikekorea.com).

Translator Profile

Robert Perron (https://robertperron.com) is the author of the novel *The Blue House Raid* and the short story collection *Wasteland and Other Stories*. His short stories have appeared in numerous literary journals. His past life includes military service, a career in high tech, marriages, and children. Today he bounces between New Hampshire and New York City, where he stays with his longtime girlfriend.